Praise for *Crossing Thres*

D1342150

"Whatever else future historians will have to say about the year 2020, it will be seen in retrospect as a year of crossing thresholds. This fact alone would make a book entitled *Crossing Thresholds* timely. But Amba Gale's book is even more timely for another reason, at this hour: In quarantine on account of the coronavirus pandemic, countless people are learning again to be enchanted by picture books, the way they used to be as children. Thus, Amba's book is coming out exactly at the right moment. Master photography and poetry like hers would have power to enchant eyes and hearts at any time. But now, our eyesight rinsed by tears and our hearts widened by silence, we are ready to be guided across inner thresholds we will have to cross before we can cross the outer ones awaiting us. Amba Gale's work can provide much needed guidance. Blessings on its task!"

—BROTHER DAVID STEINDL-RAST, Benedictine monk and founder of Gratefulness.org

"I love Amba's book, and I love her poetry. We are tuned into the same channel. I thank her for bringing such beauty and wisdom and truth into the world. *Crossing Thresholds* provides a gift of healing for all of us—individually, collectively, and globally—as we cross this threshold time, between worlds, being taught lessons by Mother Earth, who herself has had difficulty breathing. Poet David Whyte says in his poem *Loaves and Fishes*,

'People are hungry and one good word is breath for a thousand.' This is a book that will feed and nourish."

—LYNNE TWIST, author of *The Soul of Money* and co-founder of Pachamama Alliance

"To live deliberately, that's why Thoreau went to live in the woods. Amba Gale has provided an inspirational, and practical, guidebook to the rest of your life. It will help you, every day, to truly regard your life, your soul. Along the way, you may come to recognize the connectedness of all things, living and otherwise."

—ROLF O. PETERSON, author of *The Wolves of Isle Royale: A Broken Balance*

"Through a marvellous cornucopia of poems, pictures, and practices, Amba Gale precisely defines the human being's journey through life in all its manifest forms and expressions. Truly, this is the wonderful outcome and upshot of a life lived to the full. Here is an expression of the wisdom of one seeker and searcher—a DIY manual birthed from the author's insight and good judgment. Amba has fashioned a work of great transformation and healing for our troubled earth at this time. This is surely a contemporary Scripture, where every verse, every image, and every contemplation is a prayer for the universe. Franz Kafka, the Bohemian writer regarded as one of the most important figures of twentieth-century literature, wrote: 'A book must be the axe for the frozen sea within us.' Now is the time, reader, to take up this literary cleaver, *Crossing Thresholds*, and begin cutting through to the fish hole of your soul."

—The Rev. Nóirín Ní Riain, PhD, spiritual singer, author, teacher, and soul searcher

"Stunning. Wisdom-drenched. Elegant. Beauty beyond words, yet her words will lead you toward discerning a more meaningful life. Allow Amba's guidance to seep into your soul, your heart, your mind, and, maybe most of all, your eyes. Amba has been preparing for this work all of her life. Let it be her gift to you."

—Donna Zajonc, Master Certified Coach and Director of Learning and Coaching, Bainbridge Leadership Center

"I have had the privilege of seeing this book grow from a handful of seeds that Amba let me glimpse by the River Shannon in Ireland in 2018. Those little seeds of pure intention and potential have blossomed into this exquisite flower that you now hold delicately in your hands. This flower is a bridge—a vanished bridge that is brought back into the sight of our mind's eye. Each word in this book is a stepping-stone for us to skim across the surface of our soul. With each turning page we turn further toward that something that is never disappointed, and forever encourages us—*Do not despair.*"

—Owen Ó Suilleabhain, singer, composer, speaker, and founder of Turas D'Anam: Journey of the Soul

"This book can transform your life! Amba's invitation to pause through poetry, inquiry, metaphorical photography, and journaling gives each of us the opportunity to move again, to let go and journey to new places where your next threshold will advance you to greater destiny. Breathe this book into your heart. A whole new, exciting world awaits you."

—Bill Weymer, President and CEO, Town and Country Markets, Poulsbo, Washington

"The book is wonderful, some really snappy lines of poetry and a real flow through them, and the photos are stunning. I've always loved applied art projects, and this intersperses and encourages the use of the poems in context of group and solo reflection. The poems achieve the stillness and awe of the beautiful island. It is a guide for all of us to break open our hearts and the hearts of others through poetry and the yearning and personal demand for presence. Bravo."

—Mícheál Ó Suilleabhain, poet, singer, and author of *Early Music*

"I doubt there's been a more important time to acknowledge our collective 'Threshold' and to explore our own ability to self-reflect. Amba, authentically sharing tender and vulnerable moments, takes us right to the edge for a deeply personal dive. No need to fear; even as the canvas of our days change, she skillfully walks us through."

—Kathryn Lafond, intuitive healer and author of *Seasoned with Gratitude: 250 Recipes and Blessings Celebrating the Greater Nourishment of Real Food*

"I was surprised by the connection I felt, the shared awareness of how to experience physical and spiritual life, reading this book. The strength of *Crossing Thresholds* is in the words, lessons on finding meaning, and Ansel Adams would agree and applaud her use of imagery. For the photographer, poet/author, or student of life, awareness and insight are essential to defining and grasping concept. Amba's photographs are inviting portals to her island experience. Let each be an invitation to the words they inspired."

—MARK ALBERHASKY, MD, contributing photographer for NIKON, photo educator, author, and inventor

"I love this book and recommend it to you with all of my heart. It's author is a woman of rare courage and open heart. Her very personal journey, expressed so tenderly, beautifully, and powerfully in these pages, speaks to and touches our humanity in surprising, delightful, and meaningful ways. *Crossing Thresholds* reaches within us and simultaneously awakes, soothes, and inspires. This is an intimate book, at once both delicate and piercing. I relish its soulful truths and predict that, like me, you will find yourself returning to it again and again, discovering new joys in each visit."

—SANFORD (SANDY) ROBBINS, Producing Artistic Director, Resident Ensemble Players and Professor and Chairperson, Department of Theatre, University of Delaware

"One small line in any poem in *Crossing Thresholds* looms large with wise guidance for our own thresholds we are unsure of crossing, and then learn to cross with trust and courage. Over thirty-five years of knowing Amba, I have witnessed her courageous, unwavering intention to go toward her next threshold crossing in the midst of uncertainty and without formula, except for listening to her heart of wisdom—the wisdom radiating through each poem. When I read *Crossing Thresholds*, I am reminded of Rilke's advice about living into questions. Whether I'm in a dialogue with Amba, attending one of her courses, or reading her poetry, I'm always left with a profound question to live into, which has opened up my life in so many ways I couldn't see on my own. The book also returned me to my deep love of the land, and a sacred appreciation for the wisdom garnished by the poetry lived out loud by Amba. *Crossing Thresholds* is our most useful guide for today's challenges and how we can learn to listen for what life is calling for us to move toward and fulfill."

—JAN SMITH, president and founder of Center for Authentic Leadership, Inc.

Crossing Thresholds

Island Reflections

Poems, Inquiries, and Photos

Amba Gale

ISLAND REFLECTIONS
PRESS

Published 2020
Printed in the United States of America
Print ISBN: 978-1-7346941-1-6
E-ISBN: 978-1-7346941-2-3
Library of Congress Control Number: 2020906658

Use of the excerpt from "To Bless the Space Between Us," by John O'Donohue, was granted by permissions of the publisher, Penguin Random House.

For Don
whose eternal patience,
unstoppable appreciation for life,
love of the wildlands, and beauty of nature,
Musician to the Core,
Journeyer with me through the Great Work of Parenting,
and supporter as we transformed our lives through this journey.

Contents

✦ *Part III: Listening for Teachers Everywhere*

Author's Note

While this book was written in the summer of 2019, and was written around my own very personal journey, the corona virus, at this time of publishing, has brought us all into another time, another world, a time of dormancy, endings, and new beginnings. The whole planet is now in a threshold crossing.

While some of us are braving the life of service—the courageous and heroic men and women in the medical profession, the generous people in the grocery industry, the scientists, the teachers, the healing and health professionals, the wisdom thinkers who bring us into deeper wakefulness—many of us are in dormancy, in our homes, pausing, and resetting our lives.

What emerges from this time of re-set is yet to be seen. Meanwhile, if we listen, even here, in this time of uncertainty, in this time of feeling that we have no control, in this time of darkness and challenge, we can create community in new ways, we can find love in new ways, and beauty, and joy, and laughter, and kindness. We can find completion here, peace, and healing. Asking "what is the opportunity of this time—for each of us personally, for humanity, for our relationship with one another, for our relationship with the planet"—is a good question.

May this book be a voice that sends out waves of healing into our troubled land, a land and people asking to be whole, to be healed.

Introduction

—◦—

Embracing Endings, Creating Completion, and Entrance to New Starts

We human beings seem to have an addiction to certainty, to staying with what is familiar because it is safe, with what is predicable, controllable, certain. We are resistant to change, and yet, sometimes in life, we come to those special times of threshold crossings in which accepting a change of what is occurring externally while crossing inside a threshold within is *just* what is called for.

Perhaps it is a crossing to another way of being, or another way of knowing, or another way of relating. Perhaps it is, simply, a "letting go"—a letting go of a certain way of life that is changing its form, or someone dear to us who is leaving, or we are leaving them, or a letting go of a way of being, a letting go of something that once worked for us but now no longer does.

Our lives are not really one continuum, if we truly examine ourselves and notice our development, but ongoing small deaths and rebirths, if we are, indeed, committed to growing. Who we were in one iteration of our lives is not the same in the next. Once we cross that threshold into our next new life, we see the world with new eyes. And new perception means new possibilities,

new horizons, new opportunities, new presents, and new futures.

Crossing Thresholds is a transformative journaling guide. I invite you to use it that way. You can also make the journey through reflection, through thinking, through your imagination, through dialogue with another, through any form of creativity, as well as through writing.

It is my deepest intention that this book of poems, of photographs, and reflections, accompany you as a loving and wise companion, as you take your own threshold crossings. When those times in life beckon us, it is good to simply stop, reflect, and receive the teachings that are knocking at our door, asking to be let in.

This last summer, the summer of 2019, I took the opportunity to do just that. I journeyed to a magical and special place in our lives, where we live in a family cabin on an island in the harbor of a larger island, in the northernmost and largest of the Great Lakes, Lake Superior. This island is a mystery, a pristine wilderness, improbable in that small purple flowers thrive while growing out of lichen-covered rocks; loons sound their tremolo day and night, calling to one another; double suns rise in sky and lake's reflection; turbulent and wild storms light up the night sky; and in the mornings, all is still. When you are there, and you listen deeply enough, the lake can penetrate your Soul and take you on an inner journey, a journey from denial to acceptance, from resistance to being at peace.

There, on this island, it is easy to listen to the Voice of the Muse, and the Music of the Island.

It was time for me to receive the Teachings of that music, which fed me poetic lessons, and which spirited me across a threshold crossing that was mine and time for me to take.

First, I listened deeply, as you yourself may, as the natural landscape of lake and sky brought me to a Silence, a silence in which I could hear my heart, hear my future, hear the journey that it was time for me to make. These poems reflect that journey.

When I first arrived at the island, I was profoundly supported, in a threshold crossing I was committed to making, by a visual onslaught of our front dock no longer

having its bridge, the bridge having been carried away in the Spring Ice Melt; the remaining dock on its crib was left by itself, almost drowning, with the lake between it and the land. The "disembodied dock" became a metaphor for my own inner journey of coming to acceptance of change and impermanence, accepting, allowing, and even generating endings, creating completion, and starting new beginnings.

With the door of your next beginning open and the future landscape of another life, or another dimension in your life, beckoning you, threshold crossing times can be special, sacred times in our life, times of deep meaning. For, as one of the poems counsels us, "only with completion can a new beginning start."

So often, we stay in houses for far too long, houses that are filled with grief or regret for what has passed, or for what has gone, or for what or who is no longer in our lives that we wish were still there. We live in some imagined picture in our mind about how things "should" be, rather than delighting in what is there, now, for us. The opportunity of being Present in the moment to what is, and being grateful for what is—appreciative, even—is not anywhere in our purview. And yet gratitude, or even astonishment and wonder, are always present as gifts to us, waiting for us to embrace them.

Impermanence, the Buddhists say, is a Universal Law.

So, I invite you to ask yourself: "What threshold is it time for me to cross? What 'letting go' is appropriate in my life now? What coming to accept life just the way it is (and is not) is it time for now, in my life?" And, perhaps most importantly, "What is the cost for me not making this crossing at this time?"

As John O'Donohue, Celtic poet–philosopher says, in *To Bless the Space Between Us*:

"It remains the dream of every life to realize itself to reach out and lift oneself up to greater heights. A life that continues to remain on the safe side of its own habits and repetitions, that never engages with the risk of its own possibility, remains an unlived life. There is within each heart a hidden voice that calls out for freedom and creativity. We often linger for years in spaces that are too small and shabby for the grandeur of our spirit. Yet experience always remains faithful to us. If lived truthfully and generously, it will always guide us toward the real pastures."

This book is an invitation to you to live "truthfully and generously," making it your own. May the verbal and visual images in it awaken "the ear of your heart," as St. Benedict so wisely and so lovingly counsels us, and guide you toward (your own) "real pastures," your own threshold crossings.

May the poems, photographs, and inquiries, suggestions for reflecting, and "calls to action" provide you, like a guide, with an inner path that takes you deeper and deeper into your own pilgrimage, into your wisdom and your courage, your beauty and your depths, where you leave one world and come into another, a new landscape, perhaps, that you have not ever lived in before.

A few more notes before we begin:

On the Opportunity for Reflective Journaling:

I had a good teacher once, a philosopher, who used to say, "You don't know what you think until you speak it or write it." This is unusual for most of us, as we think we are merely reporting the words that are parroted to us by our brain. But, no! Perhaps there is another way of thinking, a way in which, when you go deep within, words come to you and you write what they say, and what they say speaks to you, teaches you, and even transforms you. You listen, and they guide. That is a different kind of writing, and the kind of writing I am recommending you give yourself access to through engaging with and participating in this book. That writing, if you listen to it, will take you to "new pastures."

If you experiment with engaging with this kind of journaling, with the guides of poetry, photos, and reflections, your commitment to write, itself, will forward you in descending into your own inner depth, where you connect with your own Great Intelligence, letting whatever comes to you take its shape on the blank page. Listen to your own inner wisdom and what your intuition wants *you* to know. Whether it be a meditation, an inquiry, an exploration, or an opportunity to slowly reflect, allow the words that have come to you to serve as guideposts for your own work with yourself, for your own journeying.

May they bear fruit in the sweetness that is your life. May the deep well of thought that lies within you open you to new lands of acceptance, forgiveness, softness of heart, a sense of wonder, and a profound surrender to belonging.

If you choose to experiment, explore, and engage in the adventure of your own writing, I invite you to acquire a beautiful journal, one that calls to you and your inner depths, your creativity, your imagination, as a place to reflect your own thoughts as you move through life.

Often, the questions asked present you with questions to think with, to live with. The questions are not questions to be answered, which answer then gets placed in a neat little box (which "confirmed" answer then closes down the inquiry itself), but questions to be lived, to serve as openings for new thinking, new lands to roam around in, to explore, with wonderment and curiosity, perhaps including embracing sadness and grief, depending upon what aspect of your passage the reflecting is calling up. Listen for what you and your experience have to say to you, with your heart open. "Live the questions now. Perhaps you will then gradually, without noticing it, live along some distant day into the answer," Rilke tells us.

Letting the Poems
Work with You:

Life sometimes gets messy, and it's the messiness that teaches, if we allow ourselves to experience our experience completely. So you may want to carry a poem or a question with you for a day or two or five, or think upon it as you go to sleep at night, letting it dream with you as you travel to the more invisible worlds, and breathe with you as you live through your days.

The poems are meant to flow in a certain order. If you do start at the beginning, you will be invited to move, with me, into the landscape of inner silence. Just as the Lake brought me to my own depths, that is where the Muse can meet you, as well, can come to you, inspire you, and even bring you to courage.

When I touched my courage, I saw that I could, with prayer and intention and even ease, allow myself to be transported through the difficult passage I needed to take, the passage of letting go, of ending one way of being and beginning another, of letting go of what I had been holding as certain dreams, dreams that were keeping me from experiencing the delight of what actually is, of accepting impermanence, embracing transience, and, ultimately, coming to a place of peace, belonging, and celebration. As Eckart Tolle says, "Stillness is where creativity and solutions to problems are found."

The Poems of Part I are intended to create a path for you to come to a deeper place of Stillness within yourself, from which you can tap into your own inner Wisdom, your Creativity, your Imagination, and your commitment to journeying into new lands. The Poems of Part II are poems that came out of my own journey of parenting, of letting go of a certain way of parenting my daughter, and a coming into an acceptance and profound appreciation. for who she is as herself. The Poems of Part III contain poems of further teaching, acknowledgement of others, and of meaning—wisdom I have received from the landscape of human conversation, and the landscape of the Island, that I invite you to enter into, whose land I invite you to inhabit, whose **joys** and griefs, losses and peace give you access to your own space, your own journey.

Mark Nepo says, in *The Book of Awakening*, "To journey and be transformed by the journey is to be a pilgrim."

That, I see, is our Work.

May your own work, your own reflecting, and, possibly, your own writing speak to you, sing to you, move you, touch your heart, and provide openings that allow you to be transformed by the journey.

I am grateful and privileged that this book is in your hands. May these words and visuals be a companion and guide to you in your current journey of growth, new endings, new beginnings, and the possibility of crossing the next thresholds that are yours to cross.

Blessing for the Beginning of
Our Journey Together

May the heart-breath in these poems
spirit your life
through its many journeys
to its own promised islands.

May you arrive at each inner island
as an adventurer,
    an experimenter,
        an explorer,
curious, fresh,
and ready to travel deep
into your own depths.

May you go
in accord
with your own essential nature.

May you listen with your heart.

May any heart breaks that are yours
be entered fully,
that you may receive and embrace
their lessons.

May each of your islands
welcome you with insights
and sometimes disturbing questions

that open up new territory
for you to think within.

May you be open to surprises.

May your own wisdom be a ferryman
whose boat takes you
to your next crossing
only
after you receive
the Teaching of each Island.

May you weather the rough crossings,
where the frigid wind howls and the waves grow high,
with Faith,
a great sense of not knowing,
of exploration,
of Beginning,
and a largess of spirit
that holds
your coming deaths,
    births,
        and arrivals
                    with love.

Part I:

Touching the Islands

Within Us

Reflective Journaling

Give yourself this gift to feed your Soul:
    Writing time where writing can lead
    to your own deep and hidden thoughts.
Let them come to you unbidden
    and find you as your words take shape on page.

Step aside your critic.
Let someone else write.
Let your intuition speak
from the silent corners of your heart,
transporting you to somewhere new,
Somewhere you have never been before.

Open a new door:
You are hungry for your words.

Allow yourself to be romanced
by something larger than yourself.

That's what we're all here for.

Reflection:

Imagine yourself, in reflective time, "to be romanced by something larger than yourself."

✦ *What does that question mean to you?*

✦ *What would you like yourself to be romanced by?*

✦ *What is the feeling state in your heart that that sense of your relationship to the Universe, your Inner Sprit, the Greater Mystery, the World, calls forth?*

Island, Be Our Guide

May the Spirit of the Island
benevolent and true
be our guide,
as we journal through our days.

May we listen to your Speaking,
be open and receptive:
be our guide
as we journey in our ways.

The fierceness of your gales
The gentleness of your summer breezes
May we be containers
of all paradox,
as you teach us your ways.

Acceptant, open, yielding,
we ask of you
to bring us to your language,
to your conversation,
that we may be at one with you,
inhabit you,
call you our home.

Reflection:

✦ *This is both a prayer, and a Blessing.*

✦ *As John O'Donohue, Irish priest, poet, and philosopher, tells us, in To Bless the Space Between Us, "A blessing is not a sentiment or a question; it is a gracious invocation where the human heart pleads with the divine heart."*

✦ *Let us imagine that the divine heart lives inside of you, as your own heart.*

✦ *Write your own blessing for the beginning of your journey, and your journal.*

✦ *Through your words and intention, bring down the Light of Presence to Guide you on your Way.*

Food for the Soul

I journeyed
and journeyed
until
at last,
I came to a place,
where I could step aside,
and let Something write through me.
And I found
that what I wrote

was food for my Soul.

Reflection:

Allow yourself to take a journey:

✦ *Be quiet and still, and close your eyes. Breathe deeply three or four times. Let the tension of your body ease with each outbreath.*

✦ *Feel the weight of your body in the chair.*

✦ *Now imagine yourself journeying to a place that is very beautiful, a sacred place. It could be a place you have been before, or not, outside or inside. When you are there, be there fully: take a look around; inhale the smells, notice the colors, the sights, the sounds. Notice everything in detail. Stay long enough by yourself, enjoying the beauty of this place, so much so that you feel at home here.*

✦ *Allow yourself to notice that coming toward you is a Wisdom Guide. They could be male or female, animal or human. Let them approach you slowly. Let yourself meet them, and let them speak to you. Notice they know you deeply, have always known you and who you are. They have always been with you and will always be with you.*

✦ *After you have met them, ask them a question, a question about your own journey. Hear what they have to say to you, accepting it, even if you don't understand it.*

✦ *Now, let them give you a gift, or words, acknowledging you for the journey you have been on, and offering some piece of wisdom for the present and the future.*

✦ *Say good-bye to them, knowing that you can return to this place and meet with them whenever you like. They will always be here for you.*

✦ *Write down what they have said to you. Let it be food for your Soul.*

Come to Me, My Island

Come to me, my Island,
in all your rugged beauty:
your white, rare Indian pipe,
your purple, tiny flowers growing
in the impossible crack
of orange lichen-filled rock,
hard rock, the crust of the earth,
thrust visibly out from the shore.
Lava molten, with fissure and bubble,
filled with colored gemstones.

Come to me, my Island,
with your deep, deep rest,
where, merging with the ripe
and wild spirit of all Wonder,
you give a nest of peace.

Come to me, loon call.
Like out of some mysterious other land of mourning,
you soar into my heart.
The ever-present white sparrow sings.
Magnificent, each morning.
Crackling fire, sensory feast,
in the cabin we hold dear.

Come to me,
be near to me,
as I saunter through my days
in morning haze
    and evening's glow
    and night fall's star-stud shimmering.

The sunbaked dock,
mergansers grace
the gray -white rock.
And green lake days
and old maid's face
on cliff edge steep
in North shore pace
where water's deep
and water's clear
each moment, dear . . .

Come to me,
in jack pine and birch bark,
moose leavings on the trail,
and in Great Lodge of Beaver
this year
grows fresh sprigs of green.

Come to me.

Let
your pure
Pristine
Improbable
Place
in my life
Grow into me.

Come to me.

Reflection #1:

✦ *Go out into nature: take a walk in the woods, or go to the ocean shore or lake shore. Find a place in the wilds where the sounds and sights of nature, the calls of nature touch your soul, your heart.*

✦ *Write a blessing or make a prayer that the Spirit of the Wild touch you, bring you to your own stillness within.*

Reflection #2:

✦ *Recall a time in your life where you allowed a "pure, pristine, improbable place" to grow into you, out of which you entered into a new passage, or grew in a way you would not otherwise have grown. It could be a piece of music, a particular place, a sudden storm, reading a poem or a book, a surprise in nature that greeted you, meeting a new person, having a particular conversation.*

✦ *Think upon that and who you were being, when you allowed yourself to receive such a Teaching. Let your words take shape on the page as you write about that, and bring yourself into new territory with yourself and your own inner silence.*

Where Lake Becomes Sky

Early evening:
not a breeze in this world.
Not a whiff of the wind.

Sun sets
behind the jack pine, spruce, and birch.
In water stillness,
Lake becomes Sky.

This is the beauty
 of Tobin Harbor truth.

Your boat glides, easily
cutting through still waters;
barely a sound.
Deep green trees sweep by
in the water.
Lake becomes Land,

mirror for the clouds and trees,
gray and blue and green, perfect
reflection of the world,
as the whole world envelops you
in its stillness.

Here, it is easy to see
The Whole.

When inner storms churn
 and waves
  beat
   relentlessly
at your shores,
   stirring
     your waters, fragmenting
       your ground,
may Sky reflect in you, as well.
May you find your Lake within,
filling you
with Silence.

Reflection:

✦ *Come to your own Silence, your own ground.*

✦ *Have your journal and a pen next to you before you do this meditative exercise.*

✦ *Begin with a meditation. Read the instructions first, and then engage the following visualization.*

✦ *Start with breathing deeply, following your breath with your awareness. Let your eyes become unfocused on the outbreath. Do this about eight times. You can count if you wish.*

✦ *On one of your outbreaths, close your eyes. Continue to observe, to watch your breath. If you get caught up in any thoughts, just simply note them and come back to your breath.*

✦ *Take a minute or so to scan your body, starting with the top of your head and slowly moving your awareness through your body, allowing any tension you encounter to leave your body through the soles of your feet.*

✦ *Feel the weight of your body in the chair, if you are seated, or on the floor if you are sitting on the floor.*

✦ *Now imagine being near a lake, a still lake, not ruffled by the wind, a lake where the waters run deep, and the sky, the clouds, and the land are mirrored in the lake. Continue to breathe, being with that image.*

✦ *Imagine the lake and the land inside you now as you breathe. As you breathe in, with each in-breath, allow yourself to go deeper into the still scene. Be with it. Breathe with it.*

✦ *If any thoughts come your way, once you have noticed yourself "thinking," note that you have been thinking, and just bring yourself back and be with the lake and the sky in your visualization.*

✦ *After about ten minutes, allow yourself to sense, to become aware of the physical space you are in now, and, when you are ready, open your eyes.*

✦ *After you open your eyes, and when you are ready, write anything that is yours to write.*

Beneath the Silence

This is a place for poets.

For the You in you who knows the Muse
will come
if you bow to the land,
allow your Self to grow, take your Self in hand,
becoming one with all you see.

Know your Self as the Artist.

For your love of land and lake
speaks to you, (if you listen deep),
speaking wisdom stories from
the memories you keep
and harvest.

And future visions come to you in their own glow.

This Longing lives beneath the Silence,
brings you to your inner voice and flow
of Gratitude, where you can see with clarity
what you were always meant,
always meant to know,
and what you were always meant,
always meant to be.

Reflection:

Here are two possible reflections. You are, of course, welcome to include both.

1. This is a Walking Meditation.

✦ *With intention, find a place you would enjoy walking, and walk slowly. This can be either inside or outside.*

✦ *With your eyes open, pay deep attention to the details around you. Let them speak to you. Listen profoundly.*

✦ *What do they say?*

2. Think of this Day as a Sabbath. Live in Gratitude throughout the day. Let yourself go deep, beneath the Silence.

✦ *Keep a journal with you where you write down, frequently, during the day, what you are grateful for.*

✦ *Spend some time, before you go to sleep at night, expanding your list. Be with your list. Bring yourself into a deep sense of Gratitude.*

✦ *What new insights, awareness, states of Being, open up from a place of Gratitude?*

Isle Royale Teachings

Prelude:
Nature speaks so loudly here.

1.
The sun burns hot,
and cold lake breeze
caresses my skin.

All is well without, within.

And I begin to fool myself
to think
that life will always bring me to this brink
where living will be, forever,
Just
Like
Now.

2.
Next day the great storm
Mounts its battle 'gainst the sun,
The roiling clouds race darkly over lake.
Waves kick up like Wild Horse in fear,
    hooves raised high
        and on the run.
You wonder:
Would it always be like this?

The barometer so low you'd think the sun
would never show its heat again.

The dark comes nigh.
You hear a sigh:
wind whistling through the rafters high above.

Even the fire we built won't ease us now.

In rough interior weather,
    when my soul is in despair
    and life seems so unfair,
and the roiling seas grab my mind and won't let go,
in times like these,
it is so
hard
to slow,
to listen
    to the beating of my heart
to stop,
to let Awareness meet my breath
and let the storm clouds pass.

I want to move, to throw
life around,
to make a mess,
destroy everything within my wake.

3.
Now,
    brooding stillness
        like a death
            hovers silently over the land,

smothering everything
   in stultifying humidity.
      In a life I cannot stand,
I go to sleep,
   wondering
      if the day will ever see a sun or breeze again.

During my sleep, I pray,
to be ferried to an island new,
where peace can still my restless heart.

4.
Morning comes.
  The sound of rippling waves against our island shores
     quietly make their way into my darkened doors.
  Slowly, I awake, open my eyes,
    let sun in and see another day;
      and supplicate:
May this next day be a grand surprise.
Let in this lesson from the lake:
   There is another way—
     "All will pass in time."

The butterfly will greet you when day dawns fair,
bowing in black and white in morning air,
will meet you with the flutter of its wings:
reminder of the transience of all things.

Postlude:

Fierce Nature speaks so loudly here.

The Island out, the Island in, the Island speaks in rhyme:
The Island rings in teachings from another time,
reminds us all of what is Whole in this great land
and the paradox of living in both/and.

All will pass in time.

And Butterfly in summer dress makes a Bow.
Invites us to embrace transience, and Now.

Reflection #1:

✦ *Find a place in your life currently, or in the past, where your inner turmoil has been negatively impacting yourself or others, where your actions have been unkind or ungenerous or simply based in reaction.*

✦ *Write about that. What do you see? Are you willing to accept those aspects of your own humanity that are played out when you are unaware?*

✦ *Are you willing to forgive yourself for having been that way?*

✦ *Give yourself the grace of cultivating compassion, room for yourself, and your own humanity.*

✦ *What new opening has your writing brought you to?*

Reflection #2:

✦ *Ask yourself: Where am I not embracing the transience in my life?*

✦ *Where would embracing transience bring me greater peace?*

✦ *What can I "let be" that I am not "letting be?"*

✦ *Inhabit the land of "All will pass in time." Try it on like a jacket. Wear it. Let it be a mantra for you today.*

✦ *Write about how standing in "All will pass in time" contributes a sense of settling, of calming, of equanimity, in your life.*

✦ *Allow your writing to bring you into a new space in an area of your life where your resistance to change or transience or impermanence has been negatively affecting you and possibly others.*

Where Sky Meets Lake

Melting
Into that Great, Infinite, Eternal Horizon
I want to play
I want to dance
I want to breathe
Want to Romance
I want to speak
I want to hear
I want to pray
Want to Cheer
Right
Where the Infinite
Uncurls
Uncoils
Unfolds
Itself into
The Grace of Presence:
Life
Appearing
For the
Very
First
Time.

Reflection:

✦ *Through awareness, allow your mind to reach out beyond the farthest, farthest horizon, out into the universe.*

In that great, infinite, eternal horizon,
what,
for you,
is that sense, that feeling state?

Who are you here?

✦ *Journal from there . . . just write, write, write.*

Wake up Wind

I awoke last night,
wind howling in a haunting cry,
  disturbing even
    my gentle house,
      rattling windows,
shaking me out of my slumber,

as if to arouse me from my sleep,
as if to warn me
  about complacency
    and the deep deadness
      that arrives
from a life of too much familiarity.

You awake one night,
wind howling in a haunting cry,
  disturbing even
    your gentle house,
      rattling windows
shaking you out of your slumber,

as if to arouse you from your sleep.
as if to warn you
  about complacency
    and the deep deadness
      that arrives
from a life of too much familiarity.

Reflection:

✦ *Where do you experience deadness in your life, from too much familiarity?*

✦ *Where have you become complacent?*

✦ *What are you willing to let die within you (or what has already died?) on behalf of becoming more alive?*

✦ *Where, if anywhere, are you in life not on your own leading edge?*

In acknowledgment of Parker Palmer's,
On the Brink of Everything

Heart Break

When heartbreak makes its way toward us from
the farthest horizon,
we start to close
in fear
that we will be flattened
by the loss,
never to stand again.

When heartbreak comes close like this,
we close ourselves,
never to face or feel our wounds.

The brittle heart
is easy to break.

Pain shut off and shoved aside
hides in the years,
until a time
when fearless heart we grow
and our fierce soul
takes on the past,
releases all our tears,
and heals the broken heart.

Broken open now.

Breaking open, not apart;

This is how we heal our hearts.

Reflection:

✦ Recall a time when you closed yourself off from fear of further pain, after a heartbreak.

✦ Write about that time. Notice how the whole world seemed closed off to you when you built walls around yourself.

✦ Tell the truth: notice if you still have any of those walls remaining.

✦ As the heart doesn't heal until we have accepted our pain and grieved for our loss, we remain closed off.

✦ Are you willing to heal?

✦ To heal, what must you give up? For example: anger, resentment, blame, judgments, expectations.

✦ Would you be willing to surrender, to let go of what you need to in exchange for freedom and peace?

✦ Pause, take some time.

✦ Let yourself grieve, if that is what is there for you.

✦ Whatever part of the passage you are in, take pen to paper and write.

In Gratitude for the Muse

First, I prayed for Silence,
and I was brought to Silence.
Then, I asked for you.

And you came,
enticing me
with your uplifting fire;
   hot winds blew freely through my soul.
Then, you enthralled me
   engulfed me
      invaded me
         awakened me
            to myself.

A better gift was never given.

Each morning
between sleep and wake
you entered,
giving words asked for
and not expected.

We waited in silence
together
for the sweet sun to rise

above the edge of the world,
and greet its liquid twin.

You accompanied me
 throughout my days,

spoke to me as I lay down
to sleep in my restful space,
woke me in the night to gift me
with word
images born, and made
from that other, clearer place.

On fire, I burned through days,
delighting
in my inner sun
as I rode on the water
or walked on uneven land
without, within.

Cleaning dishes in the sink,
pumping water from the lake,
showering under the thirty-gallon drum
pouring its warm rain upon my face,
hiking through the iris garden,

or to purple flowers peeking out of craggy rocks
to salute the lake,

or greeting our front dock
without its bridge.

Everything
serves as fertile soil
for the blossoming of words.

In gratitude for your arrival in my life,
I awaken each day,
praying you will stay
to kindle
the burning fire of my Soul.

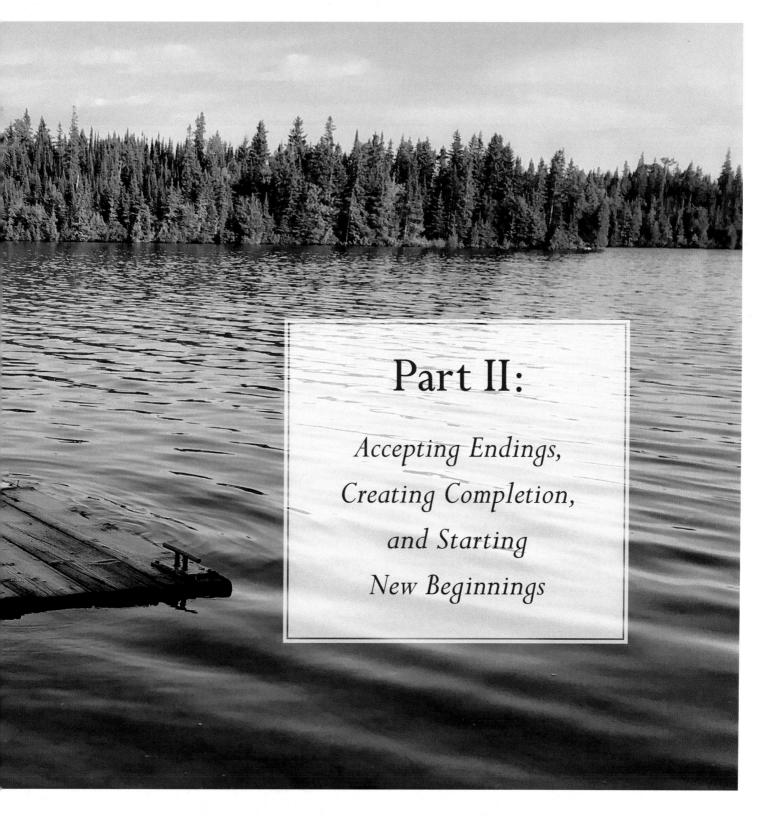

Part II:

*Accepting Endings,
Creating Completion,
and Starting
New Beginnings*

In these photographs, you can see that the dock, our front dock, has been separated from its bridge. We discovered this separation, this "disembodiment," as I chose to call it, when we first arrived at the Island this year.

The bridge had been separated from the dock when the ice went out in the spring. The dock, the bridge, and the land became a metaphor for my own inner journey of letting go of a certain way of being and a certain way of relating to my daughter. Now twenty-two years old, she is asking to be regarded and listened to as a respected adult, as someone who is responsible for her life, resourceful, someone who will and can be the author of a life she shapes that inspires her, enlivens her, fulfills her.

Along the way in our journey together, she has taught me a lot. She has taught me to let go of my attachments to a particular future, and futures along the way that I held for her and had been attached to. She has taught me to let go of my expectations for her as well, and through shedding them, I saw how damaging those expectations are across the board in my life, and that all expectations are accompanied by their flip side, disappointment. Expectations, especially those that are hidden, as most are, act as filters that keep us from appreciating and having gratitude for what is actually there. She has taught me about the importance of cultivating and creating gratitude and appreciation intentionally. She has taught me about listening, asking for a deep listening from me, with no judgment and profound appreciation, compassion, curiosity, wonder, even in the face of heartache and other internal disturbances. She has inspired in me a commitment to cross my own threshold into seeing her newly: as resourceful, responsible, and the shaper and author of her own life. I could hear during that summer that it was time to end one way of being and start another, in my relationship to her and her life.

Arriving at the Island this summer, I saw that the safety nets that my husband and I had cast had become a prison for us, a dead way of parenting, no longer appropriate, and were, in fact, deadening for us all. I saw I was being called to enter into a new field of letting go, of detaching myself from *my* intentions, my hopes, dreams, and goals, and be an open, loving, safe, nonjudgmental clearing in which she would soar, in which she could come into her own power, her own love, her own voice, her own life.

The beautiful and lonely-without-a-bridge dock became quite a metaphor, and the following poems share my inner story. May they speak to you, dream with you, walk with you.

I invite you to take yourself through your own passage, through whatever circumstances you find yourself in your own life, as you let these poems in—poems reflecting beginnings, endings, completions, stops, and new starts—and let them affect you.

The word *completion* is actually critical here. Completion means "Wholeness, Fulfillment, Lacking Nothing." You can have endings without completion, and then you are left with baggage moving into the future. You can also be complete, meaning Whole, without being finished or ended. This is a true ending, one that possibly entails a passage through loss and grief, and takes surrender, perhaps forgiveness and acceptance and creation. It opens us into a place of Wholeness and Completion, a foundation on which we can stand to create and build a New Future.

I appreciate your walking beside me as I take my journey. I am grateful to walk beside you as you take yours.

Breakaway

The cleats sink
and emerge
from the gray water clouds of the lake
as the front dock drops below
and rises
above the water line,

slow dancing with the water's surge,
the shift of wind
and the turn
of the tide.

The crib lies strong where they built her,
the interior and level right.

Only,
this year the water's high,
higher than we have ever seen on the lake.

I was not here
when it happened.

I can only imagine
at night
in the season of the year,
frozen lake and frozen dock merged as one,
marrying one another in a fusion of cold winter blast.

And when, at last,
and here, at last,

Spring began to rise.
The lake began to grow
and the sun had longer hours.
Awakening from its silent nap and snow,
moving with the outgoing undercurrent flow,
the ice began to crack,
to break,
and stole the bridge, in tow,
from its strong dock—to—shore home.

Did it shift from its bed
in one great break?
Did it make a sound when it left
its home on the lake?
Did it get carried away
in the morning bright
or in the fullness of the northern lights?
Did it wash up on another shore
where no one recognized its shape
or knew its name?

It will be seen no more by human eyes.

No matter the lore—
We do not know.

We only know this:
Do not despair.

Nature renders her surprises
as she moves
to fill the corners of the land
with her prizes:
loon song and pelicans
on the Great Lake at Passage Island
or moose and calf
near where we sleep,
sweeping my night with peaceful dreams.

Or emptying docks of their bridges.

For Nature,
in her many forms,
has her Will:
will always fill
the corners of the land.
Sweeps clean the land and lake.
Takes care of space,
adjusts for humankind,
embraces us in her grace,

and then moves on.

Reflection:

✦ *We human beings sometimes are very resistant to change.*

✦ *We get used to things being the way they are; we have the illusion of control that way, that we can navigate when the territory around us is familiar. We feel safe.*

✦ *At the same time, we do not give ourselves the opportunity to explore new worlds, new territory, new lands that way. We bury ourselves in one way of doing things: one way of hearing, one way of seeing, one way of Being, and the possibility of new possibilities does not open for us.*

✦ *Instead, we could be an opening, an "opening for Surprises," as John O'Donohue expresses it, as the surprise that occurred for us on a last night at the Island, when a moose and her calf walked onto our island and slept outside, all night, next to our room.*

So here are some questions to explore:

✦ *What is my present relationship to change? Am I willing to open myself up to changes? To transience?*

✦ *What changes have occurred in my own internal or external natural landscape that I have not as yet accepted?*

✦ *What, exactly, am I resisting? What is the cost of that resistance, or non-acceptance? (A cost is something you "pay out"—like health, happiness, vitality)*

✦ *Am I willing to move myself into a place of acceptance? (To surrender into being all right with things as they are?)*

✦ *What would that take?*

Dock's Lament

When the winter came,
like all other winters,
we lay dormant
in our white blanket of snow.

I did not know
that when the water warmed
and the ice began to crack,
in water deep,
when the lake awakened from its wintry sleep,
you would soon take leave.

I was unaware
of pending parting
until, one day, you were not here.

You must have gone easily that night.
For I, in dreamless sleep,
awoke to find you gone.

Bobbing up and down
with tidal surge
and urge of wind,
I'm empty now of boats tied to my cleats
and human feet.

I'm empty now.

What am I to do here
without the feel of human feet
to carry friends from lake to shore?
You're here no more.

You're here no more.

What is my use?

I was a home for short and for longer stays;
they used me well in all their summer days.
I was a place where neighbors came to meet,
where children sat and talked and dipped their feet.
I was a seat for viewing harbor views and lilting loon,
and in the night, the rising of the moon,
for being a place where northern lights were found.
So awed, the people viewing made no sound.
The silver slivers of the moon disappeared by dawn.
All this, until the end of summer spoke of moving on.

And now you're gone.

Alone now, without you,
what is my call?
What am I here for? Who am I for all?

Reflection:

✦ *If this poem resonates with you and some passage you are currently in or have been in the past, write down your own feelings about that space, a space where you have been left, or where someone has separated themselves from you.*

✦ *Notice your feelings; let them come up without resisting or changing them. Simply be with them, acknowledging their presence, encompassing them, feeling them.*

✦ *Create compassion for yourself, for your feelings, whatever they are; embrace them, welcome them, as poet Rumi suggests in "This Human Being is a Guest House." Let them pass through you. "Be grateful for whoever comes," he says, "for each has been sent as a guide from beyond."*

✦ *If grief for a loss is what is there for you, move into that passage, and allow yourself to fully experience it.*

✦ *When that passage is complete, see if you can bring yourself to closure.*

✦ *Allow your writing to allow you to come to a letting go of lamenting, or grieving, and being open to what's next.*

Bridge Speaks

I left at night,
and did not say good-bye.
It seemed my time.

I'm there no more.
The water high this year,
frozen in place, I took
my deep winter sleep with you.
When ice melt came,
the frozen lake embraced me,
carried me to my next shore.

Anchored to the crib on rocks,
you stayed,
while I was free to grow
into another form.

Do not despair.
For nature has a way
of wearing new clothes
as days and seasons pass.
And even
artifacts of man
(and man as well)
must go, with the tide,
when it is their time.

Reflection:

✦ *Think of a change or a death or a parting in your own life, a time when someone or something left you, or you left another.*

✦ *Are you complete and whole with this change or parting? Are you at peace? Can you embrace, without resistance, "Artifacts and Man . . . must go, with the tide when it is their time"?*

✦ *If not, sit down and do this exercise:*

✦ *Bring the person or the object in front of you, with your eyes either open or closed, and speak to it or him or her. Share honestly, from your heart, anything you'd like to say.*

✦ *Switch seats, and allow the person or object to speak back to you. Listen with your heart.*

✦ *Keep switching seats, back and forth, until you and they have said everything in your heart that is there to be said, until you are complete.*

✦ *Write about that, if you wish. Where are you now?*

✦ *If you are still not complete, explore the possibility of forgiving yourself and letting go of any regrets over that leave-taking.*

For Giving Endings

Teachings from another time are given:
All is well and "shall be well."

Live in faith, know deep in heart,
that endings soon
(in their own time)
give rise to new beginnings,
and only with completion can a new beginning start.

And I must rise to the tide of my life's calling
for giving endings where those endings are now due.

"What must I complete?"
"What endings must I cause?"
I'm called to ask.

Here, the heart can grow and gladden
with Completion's teaching:
All is Well,
   "All shall be well,
      and all manner of thing shall be well."

The Student Inside
welcomes
all the lessons from the Royale Isle
of Impermanence and Now,
of endings and new starts.

When the wild waves beat
at your shore, and in your heart, when
night lightning strikes
at your feet,
and makes a day shine from the night-darkened
porch, when
thunder drum shakes the wooden floor,
and you stumble, not seeing, as the wind
blows open all the windows, all the doors,
sweeping your house clean,
you may tumble,
you lose your hold on earth.

Know this in your heart, and let it chime the bell:
"All manner of thing shall be well."

Breathe in deep, and give it all
the space to be a part
Of Ending,
      of Beginning,
         and of Entrance
            to new Start.

"All manner of things shall be well," Julian of Norwich.

Reflection:

✦ *What is the ending in your life that it is now time for?*

✦ *What is the teaching that lives within this ending?*

✦ *Ask this question, not to get an answer, but to let the question "use you," work with you, bring you to a new light of awareness. It is a very powerful question. Live with this question for a while.*

✦ *Once you have seen that ending, what is the work you need to do to create, with completion and wholeness, that ending. Are there internal emotions to move through in behalf of coming into an acceptance? Is it grief? If it is, let the grief soften you, move through you, open and un-brittle your heart.*

✦ *If it is another passage, move through it, feel it moving through you.*

✦ *What conversation do you now need to have with yourself, or another, to start actualizing that ending in your life?*

✦ *Design that conversation.*

✦ *Sometimes, starting is the most difficult part of our work. Once we have taken our first, courageous, step, the conversation can unfold into its own fulness.*

✦ *Start that conversation.*

Lessons from the Dock

I waited all morning near the rock
to come to peace.
My sleep last night was restless.
I dreamt of wading in the water, to the dock,
to seize my fear and end it.
A new birth into another
Motherhood;
a reconciliation and a letting go
of an earlier self.

I've known that I'm the griever all along,
while writing all these poems and all these songs,
where dock and bridge speak and sing of parting,
and through which my own life does its own sorting:
not wanting her to leave the safety nest
we have built so carefully through the years
and tears
to keep her safe.

I am a sender,
a sender of new life.
And, for this, I need to be, and am,
an ender, too.

This old mode
of parenting was ours to do
for a while
in a different time,
when
she was a child.

It's hard to end who we have always been.
This threshold crossing is not so mild.

Now her years and life call forth from us a
different song,
call forth for her a new day, where she belongs
to her life:
a time to end
a time to mend
a time to bend
into a new future not yet
even
imagined.

We find we're at a new road, in the wild.
A path with no guideposts, no guide
nor instructions
along the way,
just her Speaking into Being, and us listening,
to what she has to say.

May our daughter have the gladness of new day;
a landing on a dock
she builds herself.

May we be guides
and break ourselves away
from safety nets
and nests where she can hide.
She wants to thrive
without the nets
and find her way.

And so we go, and watch, and hear her sow each day
a growing and a knowing
from the teachings that she's gained.
Each day a moving forward through another gate,
another deep,
now opened, like a wading into the lake.

When, like the bridge in icy winter break,
she, too, breaks
away
and
breaks
through
to a new,
inspired
Life,

May she wake up
to a new land
of all Possibilities.

A life based in her choice . . .
A life graced by her voice . . .
wearing the new skin into which she's grown
into a wakefulness she's not known she's known,
fulfilled, enlivened, with a happy Heart.

And with this spring, a new life starts.

Reflection:

✦ *What might be the next passage a person in your life, close to you, needs to take?*

✦ *In what ways might you empower them in making such a passage?*

✦ *Create compassion for them and for yourself as you blow wind behind the sails of their journey.*

Deeper than You Think

The wade to the front dock
is deeper than you think.

You will get wet and cold.

To stand on the front dock
and celebrate the sun,
the wind,
the blue sky
and the water,
requires some sacrifice.

Leave what is dead
and time to shed.

Leave your old life behind.

Reflection:

✦ *Sometimes it is time for us to let go of a self or form of identity that is deadening us, no longer useful to us. It might have been useful at one time and served its purpose for a while, but there are certain passages in life which we must take to step into a new life, beyond a place where we have ever gone before.*

✦ *When we cross a threshold, it may also be appropriate to let go of one environment, or one set of relationships, and move into "new pastures."*

✦ *What part of a previous identity or role or way of being or pattern or even external environment is it time for you to shed?*

✦ *What part of you or your life has already died but has not as yet been acknowledged by you as its time to grieve and send it along in its passing, just as the old bridge has left its dock?*

✦ *Take your time with this.*

✦ *Be with those questions.*

Dock's Healing

(Dock Speaks Again)

And in the cabin at the dawn of this new day,
my inquiry gives rise to a new wake.
A settling has taken place.
The lake is calm as I listen.
A new and harmonious song begins to appear,
an image starts to form and become clear:

a metaphor for one who holds me dear
for writing poems of Island life this year,

for writing poems of inner life this year.

To go on like this, I don't mind growing old,
that I may stoke the fires of her Soul.

She asks to be like lake on windless day,
serene, calm, reflective.
not riffled by the waves;
a container—
as smooth as lake holds sky—
a witness to the movement in her life,

a witness to both happiness and strife.
She must let go,
let someone near to her move on
to new life yet to come;
to break away, to separate, to go
to further shores within which Life can grow.
to know the time has come.

Honoring the past and present gifts
that life brings to the lake,
long I've grieved, it's time to mend.
It's time to bow, to bury, and to send
my memories of the past back to the earth,

celebrate them, and then move on.
Let what needs to go, go and then be gone.
Let the future be whatever shape it takes
to deeply learn the lessons from the lake.

It is here that I now know that I am whole;
I've let her see the song within her Soul.

Reflection:

✦ *"Letting go" can be very difficult. We grow attached to who we have always been, and identify with our roles and our own thinking.*

✦ *So to let go is not so easy.*

✦ *It's like holding something sharp, tight in the palm of your hand, and even though what you are holding is giving you pain, you keep holding on. To let go means to release, to open the palm, to know that you are exchanging anger, resentment, and a certain identification of who you think you are, in behalf of a new possibility, a new freedom.*

✦ *Discern what there is to let go of.*

✦ *Another way of saying this is find a place in your life where a healing is called for, forgiveness is called for.*

✦ *Forgiveness does not include "condone" or "excuse." When you forgive someone, who gets freed up is you. It is a letting go of the resentment that you are holding on to, massaging, which is like feeding yourself poison.*

✦ *Take whatever time you need, go to whatever place you need to go, speak with whomever you need to speak, let go of whatever you need to let go, in behalf of creating this healing, this new freedom, this new wholeness.*

✦ *If you are journaling, let your writing bring a healing.*

For Butterfly Emerging

(Dock Speaks a Third Time)

For breakaway to a new life,
she lets her daughter go,
and sees her newly as her Self
where new seeds she can sow. . . .

A metaphor for breakaway,
for separation's time
for transience
and being at peace
with burgeoning of rhyme.
The blessings on a summer's day,
the thoughts around her roam
for a longing for another life
where she can be at home
with newness with her daughter,
who would like for her to see
the person that she is in Truth
as she moves from "do" to "be."

To let her go, to let her live
her life as she sees fit,
to witness grace of growing
into love, and joy, and wit.

Reflection:

✦ *Think of someone with whom you have expectations, "shoulds" that you are laying on them.*

✦ *Notice that your expectations are opinions and judgments you have that you feel you have a right to.*

✦ *Notice how they suppress the other person from being themselves.*

✦ *Write down all of your expectations about that person, all your "shoulds."*

✦ *Notice that disappointment, sadness, even mourning can be triggered, as you imagine being with each person, since our ideals in our head with respect to how they "should" be and how they actually "are" do not match. Appreciation is not available.*

✦ *Imagine your expectations, each of them, like a string tied to the other person and with a pair of scissors, snip the expectations between you and them. Set them free!*

✦ *Feel how freed up they are.*

✦ *Feel how freed up you are.*

✦ *In your inner space, tell them you are letting go of each one of your expectations. Let them tell you back how that makes them feel.*

✦ *How do they feel about this?*

✦ *Now express your appreciation to them.*

✦ *Write what you see.*

Butterfly Morning

First you lit so gently on the tree
where you silently fluttered your beautiful butterfly wings
—Black and white glory—

Entranced, I breathed in awe.
Ever so lightly,
when you flew to the rock and turned
and opened your wings again,
it looked to me as though you were bowing.
A deep bow,
as we did in India,
where, with all the sacred thoughts that we could dream,
we touched our forehand to the floor,
and "pranaamed."
After, if we had been mindful,
it seemed we were in blessed reception
of all the light and energy from the earth,
and were whole,
and could bless as well.

The gift of your presence
after my uneasy night
was a blessing
and I became
an opening
for a holy day.

Reflection:

✦ *What does "holy" mean to you?*

✦ *Take at least half an hour where—out of a ritual, a meditation, a walk, a listening to music, a prayer you make, a blessing you write, a book you read, a song you sing or listen to—you create an opening for yourself for a holy day. Bring deep meaning into your day.*

✦ *Whatever it means to you, live and breathe in "holiness" and Wholeness throughout the day.*

Butterfly Spirit

Grateful,
I met you this morning
as you greeted us both
(the lonely dock and me)
from your pine perch.

Lightly, then, carried
by a mere whisper of a breeze,
you lit
on a gray-white rock,
turned,
fluttered,
and
bowed.

I could not speak.
Bowing back,
I held
my breath
in awe
of the moment,
and the world
dropped away.

No lake, no sky, no docks
No trees, no paths, no rocks.

You know inside
the cabin and the heart
that good work has been done:
the work of Butterfly Emerging.

Reflection:

This is an acknowledgment exercise.

✦ *Frequently, while journeying, and doing good work inside ourselves to grow, to transform, to create new possibilities for ourselves and others, we do not take the time to acknowledge ourselves for that work.*

✦ *If you look at your own inner movement, ground you are covering, as you move through your inner passages.*

✦ *What are they?*

✦ *What did you bring to bear to make more room for yourself?*

✦ *What, about your own work, your good work, is there for you to acknowledge?*

✦ *Let yourself take as many pages as you would like to write about this. Be generous with yourself!*

We Use the Dock!

Today, we picked up logs for fires next year
on a rocky bay on Raspberry Isle,
where the water was not only deep but clear
enough to see the rocks.
We beached the boat,
hauled a winter's catch from the long beach
into our boat through Don's long, long reach
for safekeeping back home,
until next year.

A good catch of logs, long lanky logs,
thick and heavy, ready to be split or sawed, then burned.

To drag the logs from boat to Island where we reside
was another matter.
For back dock rocky steps
are tough to climb
with tired, unsure legs,
let alone
hauling wood for next year's fires.

To get from dock to wood pile, Don got smart.
"Let's use the front," he said, instead,
thus culminating an eight-day rumination
of dock and bridge and grief and separation.

We tied the boat to a wond'rous cleat.
My thinking the whole time—how very neat
it was to have the front dock have a use.
(I know the dock's been longing for a use,
Feeling empty without a bridge,
And having no excuse to be—
No bridge to give way to boat
where we could float
or welcome guests into our home.)

And now we beached the boat near rocks and sand
and lay the logs across the bow where they could land
and be carried to the woodpile for next year.
I touched the dock with great cheer,
walked on the dock and felt the water on my feet,
as the lake is high this year,
thanked the cleat,
for giving us its safety with the docking of our boat,
and giving us the way to bring our wood into its place
on the woodpile.
Deep has been the teaching,
         deep has been the Grace.

Reflection:

✦ *Find a physical object in your life that you are about to throw away, or that has become not so useful to you.*

✦ *Reframe its purpose, so that it is eminently usable, and you love it and admire it every day!*

✦ *What new future do you now have, given this shift in thinking you have made about this object?*

Peace

I.

Serene
Silent
Still
In morning light,
Dock
Greets
Each
Day
From its lake bed.

II.

Beautiful and still in morning light,
Awakening from its lake bed
Whole, in itself, as it is,
Solitude and still.

Reflection:

✦ *Create a written expression, starting with the expression, "I am whole. I am complete in my solitude. I am still."*

✦ *In "To Bless the Space Between us," John O'Donohue wisely tell us, "Often when something is ending we discover within it the spore of new beginning, and a whole new train of possibility is in motion before we even realize it. When the heart is ready for a fresh beginning, unforeseen things can emerge."*

✦ *What new beginning, or new train of possibility, is now emerging in your life?*

Part III:

Listening for
Teachers Everywhere

"The teacher is right under our nose," is an old saying. What does this mean?

This means that if we live life in the open—ready to receive the teachings, ready to transform, receptive to life's lessons, available, and especially hungry—teachings and teachers are everywhere. If we are of open heart, open mind, open spirit, everyone and everything can be our teacher, and life's lessons are "right under our nose:" a grandmother lovingly buttering toast, the wind in the night, an experience of wearing a dry suit, a dock without a bridge.

All of life, if we look through the eyes of a poet or an appreciator of wonder, awe, and magnificence, comes to us as a metaphor.

The name for this kind of teacher, in India, I learned through Poet Mark Nepo, is *upa guru*. "The upa guru is everywhere," they say.

The poems in this section are all poems written within that frame of mind, within a way of looking at life, of being open to the teachings of another human being, the teachings of the natural world, the teachings of objects, the teachings of nature, of being an intentional listener for the tiny and the great miracles that greet us every day. Anyone or anything can show up as an *upa guru*. In this respect, even "the enemy" can show up as a teacher. Those whom we regard as "enemies" allow us to see what is inside ourselves, and see our reactions, which cause internal pressure and keep us from being fully and wholeheartedly present to what is, keep us from being free and fully alive. Once we see them, notice them, catch them, we know they are "not us" and we can disentangle ourselves from their grip on our minds and hearts. From this shift, we can create a new perspective and receive new lessons.

The upa guru is everywhere.

We start with a poem that I wrote while watching the leaves fall outside my office window, on Bainbridge Island, Washington, where, in 1999, we built our home.

Seeing the Invisible

I can see what the wind is,
the way it blows,
by the dance of the leaves.

I can see who you are,
the way you grow,
by the wake that you leave.

Reflection:

✦ *What is the wake that you leave?*

✦ *Are you happy with the wake that you leave? Does your wake leave people with a sense of being empowered?*

✦ *Think upon this: is the wake that you are leaving now the same wake you were leaving when you first began this journal?*

✦ *If not, in what ways is your current wake distinct?*

✦ *If you don't know what the wake is that you leave, what will allow you to find out?*

Listen to the Island

Listen!

Your own deeper identity,
the bare threads of your Soul,
can embrace you here,
were you to listen.

Listen
to the loon's soulful echo
of joyous connection
to All—that—Is,
to the magic music of the lake
as it laps and slaps over the rocky shore.

Listen
for the sun breaking free
of the trees in the morning.

Awaken to that other music,
the songs fully granted
from the never ending
streams of the pure, one Note.

Only you, and the natural world.
Let your imagination take you
to your own wild,
inside,
where your heart can mend
and mind can fly
free
like the eagle near
as she leaves her nest.

Leave that other life behind.

Listen inside.
Feed your Soul.
Do not
let your deeper Being
go away hungry.

Reflection:

This is a musical reverie.

Before you engage this exercise, get hungry for the following:

✦ *Find a way, (possibly through the internet), to listen to the Loon's call.*

✦ *Or listen to a piece of music you have never heard before.*

✦ *Or listen to a piece of music you love, and that moves you each time you hear it.*

✦ *Or listen to a poem, or your baby's cry.*

✦ *Listen to something that moves you.*

✦ *Take a walk and listen to the flowers, the grass, the trees speaking to you.*

✦ *Let it transport you to wherever it takes you.*

✦ *Write about the place to which you have been transported.*

Listen For The Unexpected

Be a clearing!

An empty vessel
in which you can
hear and taste
the future
filling you
with miraculous and astonishing surprises,
the unexpected:

Musical food for the Heart.

Now filled,
now
your Being being the future,
take your first step,
        befriending the unknown.

Reflection:

✦ *There is an ancient story told, to illustrate the principle of Beginner's Mind. It is said that two brilliant physicists journeyed far to visit a wise sage, a Zen master, asking him to give them all the wisdom he had.*
Without speaking, he began to fill a cup of tea and poured and poured and poured.
The tea spilled over the cup.
Finally, he said to them, "Your mind is like this cup. Come back when it is empty."

✦ *Practice living this day with Beginner's Mind, being hungry, being a call for, the Unexpected . . . being an Opening for Surprises.*

✦ *Write: What is it to live life, being an Opening for Surprises?*

✦ *Listen for a Meaningful Future, a future filled with Healing, Joy, Fulfillment, and Grace.*

The photo is of Keith Taylor, the Artist in Residence, a poet, who came to Isle Royale in the summer of 2019.

His poetry is very beautiful, and he was a strong influence in my own reception to the Muse while at Isle Royale in 2019.

Upon Reading "Summer Teaching"

For Keith Taylor, Artist in Residence Poet, summer of 2019

Reading by the fire in early morning,
  your voice sings me into your world.
    Your words are true.

All around the cabin,
  the gray wind stirs the trees,
    and rain makes puddles on our paths and plans.
The orange fire reaches up the chimney,
  stretches shadows on the walls:
    staccato in my ears.
The fire and your words are hot,
  illuminate the ordinary,
    throwing shapes in the corners
      of my mind
        that I had not seen before.

I am sorry you are leaving in three days
  this place that time declined to change.

I will still have you with me through your words
  in *Bird-while*, your book of poems, teaching
    me everything I need to know.

Reflection:

✦ *Journal about someone in your life who has been a Source of Creativity for you, of Wisdom, or who has opened you in new ways. Write about what they have been instrumental in contributing to you.*

✦ *Take some time to think upon the possibility of sharing with them what you have seen, through their contribution to you, sharing your gratitude and appreciation.*

For Keith

Artist in Residence at Isle Royale

Your simple words
crash through like waves
in fire-bright night,
singing me awake.

The image of children,
in "Summer Teaching,"
turning into trees
stirs my Soul to light,
bringing me at stake
for living a life I had not lived before.

Reflection:

✦ *Reflect upon someone in whose Presence your Life was so vastly influenced, or empowered, something new opened up. Possibly, even, you reshaped your life. It could have been one line of a poem you read, or being with a poet, or in a workshop you took, or in a one-on-one conversation with a wise sage, a peer, a friend, a teacher (perhaps they all mean the same thing, if you are listening for being contributed to) . . . and as a result of that one conversation, some inight you had led to new action, or a new path opened for you to take, and, suddenly, you had a new life.*

✦ *Write about it.*

For the Artist in Residence

(For Keith Taylor)

Your white beard
and blue eyes,
(both straight and true)
engage with me
as if
I, too,
might have
Something real to say.

May we all
see and hear
each other
in Just
      This
           Way.

Reflection:

✦ Think upon listening to others in your life with honor, with regard. Notice that with some people, you already think certain thoughts about them that are judgmental, or that you see them through the filter of your opinions and judgments or your expectations of them, that they should be some way other than the way that they are.

✦ Notice that, when you find it, as it is the automatic way of being all of us have. It goes along with the mechanistic, survival-oriented part of being human.

✦ As soon as you see that, you can choose to simply let that way of thinking about them go. Drop it. Create, instead, a different kind of listening for them, where you know that they, like you, "have something to say."

✦ Listen for their beauty, their magnificence, their wisdom. If you listen for that (where the word "for" means "in behalf of"), you'll hear it . . . the wisdom. Listen for them as a Teacher. As a Teacher, what are they saying to you?

✦ People are profoundly wise. I promise.

✦ Explore listening in just that way . . . for people's authenticity . . . for people's wisdom.

✦ What have you discovered?

Buttered Toast

(In honor of Ron Nakata)

Each morning,
his grandmother's ritual
greeted his day.

The buttering of toast
was not
a task to be done,
but a bonding
of generations
of past and future,
a Teaching
of the family way.

First,
after the toast was made,
she'd butter the toast
perfectly
evenly, smoothly, consciously, richly:
just enough and not too much,
the corners perfect:
no area untouched
by the delicious smoothness
of the butter.

He watched, entranced,
as she took her time,
the time it took

to butter the toast. . .
perfectly.

At last, when the toast, itself,
sang of its miraculous completion,
the knife came out
to slice
diagonally, evenly, smoothly
Perfectly,
but not quite through the toast,
making almost—but not quite—two
very perfect pieces of heavenly goodness.

"That way," he said,
"when you pick it up,
you get a whole slice."

Umami.

And
he'd snap it in two and
attentively, slowly,
savor the feast
of the buttered toast:
the wholeness
the buttery, toasted goodness,
and mainly the love,

the love that came from
his grandmother's heart,
feeding life itself,
speaking to us all
from beyond time
through the gift
and her teaching.

"Small is great,"
he says,
teaching us *umami* ways.

And we all receive, and feast,
savoring,
tasting,
the unstinting giving
of love beyond love,
of our grandmother's
buttered toast.

Reflection:

This poem gives an opportunity for, at least, four reflections or actions.

1. Take an ordinary, everyday action that you perform and bring an attentive, super-focused, loving Presence to it, bringing it and yourself into a wholeness, a "perfection."

✦ Later, write about your own sense of amazement, wonder, delight, in having performed this action.

2. Find something "ordinary." See it as "extraordinary."

✦ Let the grace of this ordinary thing transport you into full delight.

3. Get a book of Mary Oliver's poetry. Mary's poetry brings us fully into the extraordinariness of the everyday. Read one poem each morning. Let that become a practice, a ritual, for yourself, to begin your day.

4. My friend, Ron, shared with me that his grandmother's toast buttering is, essentially, a poem about Love as the Source of True Service, in action, in the world.

✦ Inquire into the question, "What is it to live from True Service?" What does that provide you and others?

✦ Find, and live in, the gift that that opportunity is . . . and let it in.

Faith

Faith
is a wet suit
I wear
when I go rafting
in the icy waters of the world.
Life sometimes serves up rapids
that would have us drown in their glory
on their desperate flight to the churning sea.
Tumbling over boulders, they make their way
through the wild lands,
quenching our inner flames,
as the fierce winds blow and the mighty rivers churn.

I am humbled by this life,
brought to my knees,
sometimes
broken.

Yet,
when I surrender,
when I pray for light,
faith,
like a wet suit,
holds tight my body,
wraps me in my inner warmth,
and carries me home.

When I have nothing,
when my eyes cannot see
my ears cannot hear
my voice cannot speak
and the world is cold,
dark and dangerous,
it is all I need.

Reflection:

✦ *Reflect upon the Nature of Faith.*

✦ *What is it?*

✦ *What is it not, but confused with?*

✦ *What does it allow for?*

✦ *What is your access to it?*

✦ *Lean into it and see what opens up.*

Barometer Teachings

If it goes to the left, we stay inside
with rain and thunder and the moving tide.
if I move the needle to the right (and could)
It means the weather in sight is so darn good!

Reflection:

✦ *Regardless of the weather outside, check your weather inside.*

✦ *Where is your barometer needle located?*

✦ *What is the conversation you need to have with you to move your barometer needle to the right, where the weather is fair?*

✦ *What new Possibility can you stand for?*

✦ *Create or design that conversation.*

On Raspberry Island

The improbable, impossible fissure
in the rocky outcropping
gives
a home
to as yet
a more
improbable, impossible
  shy and sturdy
  timid and true
    Purple Flower.

It springs
from the rock
out of nowhere
on this improbable, impossible island,
speaking to me on this sunny day:
"If I can grow here,
So can you.
If I can sow here,
You can, too.
What do you sow
When the cold winds blow?

Here, life is true."

What does The Flower
say to you?

Reflection:

✦ *Look at the photograph. Listen to the flower speaking to you. Write down what is says.*

✦ *What does The Flower say to you?*

Twice Golden

Twice Golden, the sun
 Breaks,
  opens,
   above the horizon line,
    where Lake meets Sky.

Twice Golden, lake and sky,
 each morning:
  twins.

The sky's Golden Orb twice celebrates the awakening
 of the day,
  slowly rising above the light-filled pines.

Imagination awakens,
 paints the lake in all its colors.

Each day, the canvas changes,
 depending solely on the lake,
  the waves, the wind, the weather, and the tide.

No morn is same as last.

Each day,
 we're taken on a ride
  by the sunrise.

May we be Present
   to the Eternal Now
      of Sunrise Brilliant Golden
      and Glorious Radiance
coloring the sky
   painting the lake
      celebrating all the vivid hues of the world:
Pink, Orange, Yellow, Golden, Green, Purple, Teal, Navy, Turquoise—
All of it here,
         All of it now,
            the new Sunrise awakening
               the rise of the Imagination, soaring, high above the treetops,
            the lake as its canvas.

Pick up your pen, pick up your paints, pick up your brush,
   Let your World be your Canvas,
      and Celebrate!

Reflection:

✦ *Find one of your favorite images in this book, an image that opens you to Celebration. Let yourself be drawn into image. Go deep into the image. Write from your depths.*

or

✦ *Imagine something that is happening right outside the frame of the image you have chosen. Take the lid off and just write, write, write, without censoring. If you want to, you can turn what you have written into a poem or short story.*

or

✦ *Pick up your pen, your pencil, brush and paints, your crayons, your guitar, your voice, or whatever creative medium you like, and let the world be your canvas, and celebrate!*

Wild Iris

You
can't go anywhere
from here,
except inside,
growing
on the bank of the lake, as you are.

Always listening to the wind and water,
your thoughts must grow so deep.

Share with us, please,
so we can think your thoughts
and go deep, like you.
Your face is lovely.

How rich must be your dreams.

Reflection:

✦ *Focus in on the wild iris photos.*

✦ *Breathe slowly. Imagine the Wild Iris is taking you deep.*

✦ *What is the Iris dreaming?*

✦ *Listen for your Heart and what it says to you. Write that down.*

Superior Symphony Storm

Movement One: Allegro

We started out to the back dock
with anticipation
of the arrival
of the coming storm.

Halfway there, we stopped,
taking caution as our guide.

The almost blinding flash
  lit up the dark
    and stopped us in our movement
      toward the dock.

One split moment after—
a syncopated beat—
  the blinding flash that swam across our eyes
gave way to such a sound I have not heard:
a cymbal crash
through speaker
only nature could conjure.

The violent clash
ripped
through summer air
and sent us scurrying back to our back porch.

The symphony has been well begun;
a musical ride for us to take:
peels of sound and sight out on the lake.

Movement Two: Adagio

Front porch.
Safe.
And here we stay.
Listening and breathing with the wind
dancing through the trees,
listening for the sounds of the leaves
and the steady breeze.
Wind chooses her own path,
makes her own rhythm.

Movement Three: Vivace

Next, night lightning fork strikes
our sight once more,
brightens all the grey, white clouds
as if it were the day. Deep notes resound.
Percussion players follow right away,
never stopping for a breath as they
roll right through the harbor shores
drumming all the way.
The thunder rolls—thrums,
its deep throated sound
like a "basso profundo" in our hearts.

And the banging of our cabin doors
joins
these spirited sounds;
the movement down the harbor brisk and wild,
composing a night rich with sound and light.

Movement Four: Largo

In the cabin now, by window wide,
with images of Dragon Isle,
when sky lights land like in a summer's day.

What I hear is fire crunching,
eating hungrily the wood,
behind me,
lighting the cabin
orange with its flame.

Then,
   slowly,
      falls
         the rain.

Soft and slow, the movement:
You hear it:
brushes on a snare drum
on the roof
on the ground
in the once
glassy lake
on the lichen
and the branches of the trees.

There is no wake, no swell.
No boats come here tonight.

We're glad we're home.

The healing house provides safety and balm.
While the storm is not quite gone, it starts to calm.

Prokofiev, even,
as wild as he was,
could not have composed
this symphony so well.

Reflection:

✦ *Pick a time this week to spend some time outside. Take your journal with you.*

✦ *Find a comfortable place to sit.*

✦ *Allow yourself to breathe deeply, and slowly. Close your eyes. Listen to the sounds around you. Watch your breathing for a while.*

✦ *After a while, allow your eyes to de-focus, and gently rest on the landscape, the weather, the cityscape, what you see, what you hear, what you sense.*

✦ *What kind of music does this external landscape remind you of?*

✦ *Pick up your pen and write freely.*

Tobin Harbor Haiku

On the tail of the dragon
Slowly emerges a white dot:
A cargo ship.

Reflection:

✦ *Haiku is a traditional form of Japanese poetry, consisting of three lines. The first and last lines have five syllables each, and the middle line contains seven syllables. Usually, the lines do not rhyme.*

✦ *Write a Haiku about something in your life, internal or external.*

Preface to "The Song of Belonging"

The year was 2003. It seemed like a normal morning on Isle Royale, a day in which the Artist in Residence and his two sons were coming over for dinner later that day.

Of course, that meant serving food for six. We thought fish would be perfect.

So, off we went fishing on a day that looked like any other.

The Song of Belonging

We caught two fish today,
my daughter and I,
to serve at dinner.
My husband worked to secure the catch, net in hand.

He always has a net.

Hard they fought,
and hard we reeled,
excitement and fierceness
in the air we breathed,
as we brought our single focus
to the fish
on our lines
for dinner that night.

After the fight,
later that day,
fish having been played,
Philip, the Resident Artist,
graces our home
with his sons, wide in age.
Mathew and Graham,
zucchini in tow
for our great fish feast.

They did not know our cabin home.
  Wide-eyed, the artist and his young sons
  listen to the old song
  of history past,

told by my husband:
Grandmother
in wide-brimmed hat
and bustling large skirts
cheerily
making fresh-squeezed orange juice
in her kitchen dear
as the brothers and cousins
frolicked in the back room,
making noise,
knowing even then
how special a time this was.

They built their home on an island:
the family cabin,
Grandmother and her sons,
where moose tracks and drippings
line the trails,
and Dragon Island looms forever
in the sun-speckled lake: view from the front.

On a small three-acre island,
in a harbor of the Lake
in the midst of Tobin's wilderness
where very little wake
creates a graceful dance of stillness.

A superior romance
between trees and water
humans and lake

was borne, takes shape:
fishing and boats,
friends and floats,
thirties style;
while all the while,
history in the making.

These stories all appeal
to their artistic ear.
And a sense of history
prevails,
throws a glow
around the cabin
as the young boys and artist sail
    into pictures of time past.

Ears and eyes wide open,
imagination soars as we prepare
the fish, greens and zucchini—

Jaws dropped, they see
the pots and pans hanging
from nails on the wall,
the dishes and silverware clanging,
they hear the call—
of the primed red pump,
the great artery here,
up and down and down and up,
creaking, squeaking, the only way the pump speaks,
springs and sings and brings lake water clear,
lake water dear.

The orange juice maker,
cleverly
circles
round and round its fruit,
yielding the sweet pungency of liquid orange.

Wide-eyed,
the older brother
smiles at the toaster,
which gently accepts the bread
in its open arms
as it rests upon lit stove.

Entranced by the magnetic strip
for kitchen knives,
the younger comments, smitten.

Interest in history spawns
questions allowing for revelation,
questions tumbling,
one by one, each by each.
In this way, we make our way
through connecting speech,
and conversation.

Entrancing them with stories from the past,
we gladly address their queries.

"You are as much a part
of this place as the trees and grass,
rocks and soil,
loon and seagull,
fish and lake,"
The Artist speaks.
Below us, the tide goes in and out.

Benign sounds of little waves lap on the shore,
as we sip and eat and laugh on the wide-screened porch,
seeding conversation.

Suddenly, a disturbance:
the loon's frantic call,
one song followed by another,
all high tremolos,
a song for taking caution—
a longing for safety.

The seagulls, too, join
the fearful calls,
adding their high pitch
and percussive sound to the mournful,
fearful melody of the loon,
now flying hither and yon,
like some great wind has unsettled their nest.
like some great God has disturbed their rest.

All the birds and trees of the kingdom
seem to take a part,
as though a violent and terrible storm has arisen
on this graceful day.

Our human voices join
as we gradually become aware
of the Great, Mysterious
disturbance in the air.

Quizzically, we look to one another,
question the dissonant symphony of sounds.
"What is this?"
"What is this unsettling?"

And, then, a break to understanding dawns
as Mathew the Elder points to treetop.
"There! "he says, as our necks swivel upward
"There," he says, and we come to a stop.

Startlingly, surprisingly, smoothly
swooping swiftly south
down
to the land
soars the eagle,
harassed by the seagull.
at his tail.

A new theme on its wing,
a new rhythm in the mix.

"Ah!" we say,
our understanding joins the chorus of voices.

Another magnificent glide to the sky
above the lake
where Eagle can fly.
And below, on the lake,
before eagle can fall,
with all the distress a loon can call,
a tremolo mourns
or warns
through its song
as the seagulls cry.
And all the creatures of this
greenly treely island home
disturb the silence.

At long last,
as the eagle dives,
takes one last chance,
Mother loon cries—
in one great, clean leap—
for protection's sake,
engaged—flaps her wings—
Enraged, wages war,
war that only a Mother can make.
That is what Mothers are for.
And with Great Care,
ascends ten feet from the lake into air.

Eagle turns
Off
And
Flies
Away.

And we felt
that Something had ignited within—
fire in our hearts,
awe in the grandeur,
wonder and gratitude
of that glorious moment.

The tales that were told
of family and friends,
and Northshore fish,
boating on the island,
of home and family,
paled
in intensity

to the Great Surprise of nature,
that swooping presence of glory.

Our own heart fires kindled, awakened
by the sight and sound of such a swoop,
and the fierce, fighting beauty of Loon and Eagle
in all their final revelatory fight
of one, final leap
Ah, such a sight!

And we?
Almost left spent
with gratitude
for the gift
of belonging
of witnessing
such hot-blooded grandeur.
The tenseness of such momentous fierceness
and later, much later,
the presence of peace.

Our Brotherhood with the Eagle and the Loon
brings with it
our brotherhood with all living things.
And the question, "Do we belong here?"
announces its ludicrous irrelevancy.

Perhaps, just perhaps,
"To What do we belong?"
becomes the Question
in the Presence of such fierce and fiery song
of nature,
all in the process of Nature Being
wholly herself.
Perhaps that
is the guiding question,
As Eagle, Loon, Seagull, and Man
take their place
true to the pattern
true to themselves,

where the song
of every single atom
of creation,
of the lake and trees,
fish and birds,

celebrates Life and Death
in the making
and awakens our sensibilities
to the bigger Question of Life:

To What do we Belong?

Reflection:

✦ *To What do You Belong?*

Nature: The Artist at Work

Dark storm clouds
pour
  down
    gray
      rain,
Intermittently,
insistently.

Flag Island it is named.
"Dragon" is its fame, and shape,
throughout the youthful years.

Rain pours down his lengthy back,

a moving painting to bless a rainy summer's day.

Now, on the head,
Rain, gray rain, stops a while,
and washes all the worry from his mind.
We watch, we smile,
as the ever-changing canvas of the sky
glides swiftly past the head, like on a smooth skidded runway,
rain everywhere.

And, intermittently,
the sky above
paints itself in blue
among white and gray clouds,
blankets the sky
with soft imaginings
of ever rearranging shapes.

The canvas of the clouds
ever moving,
    ever changing,
        ever shifting,
shapes which reshape

Intermittently.

Moving canvas
touches only lightly
on the canvas of my mind.
Intermittent thoughts
come and go.
Rain so slow,
nothing stays
in one place
for any time
on this day.

Like Dragon tears
may my fears
may my thoughts
may my tears
may my "oughts"
come and go
in just this way.

Reflection:

✦ *Take fifteen minutes to engage a meditation:*

✦ *Close your eyes. Notice your breathing. Let your awareness follow your breath.*

✦ *Practice Being the Blue Sky, the Canvas, on which your thoughts, emotions, feelings, like clouds, drift past. Notice them, touching them lightly.*

✦ *Notice when you have gotten entangled in the cloud, like it's real, not drifting, ever-changing. When you noticed that you have noticed, let go and come back and focus on your breath.*

✦ *Practice being the sky.*

Packing Day

Morning now,
I gaze out on our boat
floating on the lake,
tethered to dock and rock
by ropes tied fast.
The front dock plays hide-and-seek
with the water,
half in the lake, half out.
Meaningful to me, as it gave me days
and ways of thinking, and of being
in relation to myself.

I too
will be out soon.
Half out already,
as images of my other life
appear to me
as I begin to pack.

Today,
our last day here,
we choose to boat down to Hidden Lake.
A young girl greets us upon arrival.
Grateful, I think she's on the dock to tie our ropes.

That is not the purpose of her greeting.

She starts to talk upon our stop, meeting
us with friends nearby, to plea
for any new and unseen thoughts
for retrieving her cell phone, which she
has dropped into the lake.

Wanting to serve,
Don was so taken
 with the fervency of the request,
he quickly docked.

Pointing to two oars
to lift the cell phone
from its place between two rocks,
we left them to their musings,
beginning our hike up to Hidden Lake.

Picnic table near the iris
near the path at Hidden Lake
made a spot for our tuna picnic lunch.
All was quiet way down the path by where we docked.
After lunch, the happy whoops and hollers of the teens,
celebrating,
let us know the cell phone
had been retrieved.

After lunch we took a walk around the lake.

The purple and yellow iris looked at us with surprise,
their eyes wide with smiles on their face,
happy to harmonize
our own welcome with theirs.
Next to gray lake, loving being seen.

Moose grazed on green grass across the way
near the Beaver Lodge.
No beaver slapped the smoothness of the lake.

Beaver dam's now bigger than last year.

Later, that same day,
after packing was complete,
we walked to the lake shore at our back dock.

The back dock, sun-filled, warm, we find a seat,
look out on the lake, take in the heat:
Mother Loon is feeding her young one.
Filled with wonder,
we watched and watched
as loonling fed from Mama's beak.

In this repose, we're grateful for
the Sabbath of this day.
We've stopped and moved outside of time:
blessed ending to our Stay.

Reflection:

✦ *Each year, packing day is a special day at Isle Royale, knowing it is our last time for being in this particular wonderous environment for a year. We always want to "pack it all in," so to speak, on packing day.*

✦ *So this poem, like that day, has a lot of passages, a number of external journeys, apparently not related, except for the depth of meaning that we chose to live with through the day.*

✦ *Today or tomorrow, imbue your life with awareness of the details in it, with receiving lessons from all who touch you and all whom you touch, finding meaning in what you behold and interact with.*

✦ *Let yourself be blessed by the ordinary.*

✦ *Write about that.*

Watching in Wonderment

From our two-chaired back dock sitting place (as comfy as a lawn),
the sunlit wakes, way across the lake, is how we see them.
They are here, now there, now gone.

My husband's crocs and gray socks rest light
as we hunger to keep the wake within our sight.

They're small; too small to really catch a glimpse,
our eyes no match for seeing past this great distance.
We do not see them—only their wake—
in the green soft stillness of the tree-colored lake.
As we seek to join them in their afternoon,
we bring out the binoculars to see them soon.

Brown, small fluff floats lightly on the lake,
loonling feeding in deep water green;
only ripples, in this still water scene.

Fish shifts from loon's beak to loonling beak,
Mother and the little one, who seek to seek
their fish for food, with no air in between.
The fish she brings up from lake are small and lean.

Under the water she dives again, her work is done.
And up she comes, breaking the surface, feeds her young.
Beak to beak.

Male loon mate down the harbor hails.
Female, in quick response, wails,
a second or two between the timely beats
though in their calls there is no sign of fear.

(We do not hear a tremolo right here.)
"Where are you?" the male loon calls.
"I am here," immediate, her song, in the return,
as she paddles with her strong unswerving feet
answering her mate, now, beat to beat.

He knows their young one's near.

And as the ever-setting sun moves toward the west,
we join the loons enjoying their feasting quest
for two hours, though time moves slow upon great lakes,
and all is Still and Now: we watch three wakes.

From our back dock,
for Beauty's sake,
beak to beak
adorns the lake
with their strong song
and their long call.
We watch in wonder,
enthralled,
by it all.

Reflection:

✦ *Cultivate within yourself a capacity to listen, to be with the world, through the eyes of wonder.*

✦ *Take a walk.*

✦ *Allow yourself to be enthralled by what you see.*

✦ *Afterward, write about your experience.*

Where Lake Meets Sky

Look beyond yourself.

Look first to the farthest horizon where
lake meets sky,
and then, even farther.

Take
one easy paddle toward that horizon
and notice
how the wake appears,
then disappears,
behind you.

Pilgrim,
You must not go back.

Only the open lake
in front of you
with no shoreline to mark your way.

Listen with your heart.
Your heart knows the way.

"The happy heart is true,"
St Brigid speaks.

Follow your joy.

I know you can live wholeheartedly,
that you can be who you choose to be.

I know
that you can paint your life
with the palette colors of your choice.

I know that you are the author and the artist of your life.

Listen,
and paddle toward your Voice
calling to you
from across the lake,

from the endless horizon where
lake meets sky,
from the eternal
Infinite
Possibility
of All—That—Is,

the Voice that calls you by your name.

Come home to your Self.

Reflection:

✦ *What is your farthest horizon?*

✦ *What is just beyond the farthest horizon?*

✦ *What is your True Name?*

✦ *Live with St. Brigid's Teaching: "The happy heart is true." What does she mean?*

✦ *Are you willing to live into the Infinite Possibility of All–That–Is?*

Build Your Home on an Island

I.

We built our home on an island,
a Northwest, bountiful Island,
where the still and gray waters
of the Salish Sea
embrace our home,
cleanse my soul,
and mirror the dark gray storm clouds above.

My heart listens to the liquid conversation,
a Northwest conversation,
honest and real,
deep and abiding,
between shimmering sea and glimmering sky,
between pine-scented forest and salt-swelled tide,
transient
real
dying
reborn each moment of each day.

No wave is like the last.

Each dies as it lies down upon the shore.

I hear the waves of wild and calm,
sorrow and joy,
grief and exuberance,
calling me to welcome them,
begging me to live a life fully lived,
a life that I create and truly call my own.

Sea
converses with Mountain.
Mountain
converses with Sky.
Sky
meets the water gladly.
Water
kisses the wind.
Wind
dances with the trees.
Trees
welcome the tumbled and tossed wild flowers,
who bow and nod to us
who bow to them.
Gazing out our windows
we feel this wild beauty,
creating Sabbaths in our lives.

I, too, rest in this Sabbath,
am drawn by the rhythm of the earth
and the cascading beauty of the land
down to the sea.
I have come here, to this place,
to build my home.

II.

Our home:
A place of belonging,
sourced by the echo
of another summer island
in the Great Lake of this land,
where the sounds of eves
and days,

of trees and bays,
and the raw turbulence of the wind
whooshes wildly,
dances delightedly,
with the ever growing, glorious, prancing waves.

I can hear
the sun setting
over Canada,
while the rose-dappled lake
welcomes our evening sail.

And the woodshed,
now ochre in the evening light,
bursts with wood the brothers have gathered
from forgotten beaches,
where winter logs have washed ashore.

Stacked
for our evening fires.
Long into the night they burn.
Ah, Pilgrim!
The Isle is another story, indeed.

Meanwhile,
meanwhile,
take the journey.
Find your Island within,
your own wild and sacred place,
inside;
the place that calls your name.

The path untrodden
where the wind carries you
to your own deep listening,
the Island in your heart,
where you finally,
finally
come
to that surprising place
where your awareness meets your breath
and you are still.

"*Ruach*," the Hebrews named it,
the Spirit-Breath,
the wind
that breathes Stillness
Into Life,
takes us to the Island within,
where love meets a happy heart.

And the changing tides
do not disturb this peace,
the Presence of this place
called Now
the Presence of this place
called Here
the Presence of this place
called Love.

III.

Build your home on an island,
a beautiful, bountiful island
where the still and blue-green waters
welcome you home,
embrace your soul,
and mirror the sky above.

And the wind carries you,
ferries you,
to that place,
to Love.

Reflection:

✦ *Be still. Allow your awareness to follow your breath. Focus inward, following your breath. Imagine yourself with a happy heart. Feel your heart's happiness expanding out through the universe, touching everyone with happiness, with joy, with compassion, with Love.*

✦ *When you open your eyes, if you wish, write down your experience.*

✦ *Ask yourself:*

✦ *What is the Name of Your Island Home?*

✦ *What has been your new, inner arrival, as you have taken this journey?*

✦ *What new possibility or possibilities have opened up for you through your own reflecting and writing?*

✦ *What have you left behind?*

✦ *What new openings are you now standing in front of, having journeyed to this still, inner place?*

For Whom I Am so Grateful:

"Nothing gives you more joy than when your heart grows wider and wider and your sense of belonging to the universe grows deeper and deeper."
—BR. DAVID STEINDL-RAST

So many people have contributed to my foundation, and, ultimately, to the expression that is this book of poetry. With each contact, with each person, my heart has grown wider and wider.

I am deeply grateful to each.

For direct contribution toward the writing and completion of the book:

Don Gale, my husband, to whom this book is dedicated, who introduced me to Isle Royale, and whose constancy of support, profound empowerment, wise counsel, partner in parenting, and creative spirit, has constantly kept me on my toes and on the edge of my own creativity. His ideas for the poems, his edits, and his photographic contributions, profoundly forwarded the voice of the book.

Ruth Blaney, my dear friend and collaborator in transforming the lives of so many, who provided me with such wise input, profound validation, ideas for writing and editing; who walked with me as I thought and wrote and revised, provided me with partnership and companionship with the book's birthing, every step of the way. Words cannot capture how grateful I am.

Pat Colgan, whose own creative spirit stood by my side throughout the process of revising, whose input and inspiration graced me along the path of bringing the book into existence, and who validated the poems, my own thinking about the flow, and the prose, throughout the process of creating the book.

Kathryn Lafond, whose sacred clarity and depth of seeing and hearing behind the veil supported and healed me through my father's death and this book's birth. Our sacred work together allowed me to break free into an opening for discerning the highest integrity and most inspiring way of bringing this book into existence.

Tim Connolly, a publisher and friend, who first got me to understand the possibility of how critical the journaling opportunity of *Crossing Thresholds* is to the overall transformative experience of the book.

Brooke Warner, my guide, coach, cheer leader, supporter, who graciously and patiently worked with me through the paths of "birthing" the book, and who made the publishing journey as much an inspiration and a joy as the creation of the book itself. Tabitha Lahr, a brilliant, creative graphic artist who lovingly gave shape to my words and photographs. Krissa Lagos who provided polishing and refining to the poems and prose, as she engaged the clean-up work of catching errors that might have tripped up the reader. Fauzia Burke, my launch coach, whose patience and unending support and encouragement have spirited me on my journey of making this book real and into the hands and hearts of many people.

A number of my clients, and friends, who have been deep listeners, deep receivers, and deep thinkers, contributed to me over many years, in my growth as a coach, teacher, writer, and poet; and have forwarded me in making this book real: Susan Allen, Bill Weymer, Larry Nakata, Ron Nakata, Joel Larway, Rick Pedersen, Jim Huffman, James Bailey, Jan Smith, Rich Duncombe, DW Green, Eric Cress, Victrinia Ridgeway, David Matheson, Pete Ophoven, Mary Harrigan, Dave Ghirardelli, Somik Raha, John McGowan, Susan Keith, Jason Parks, Tom Gale, Barbara Ludlum, and Donna Zajonc.

My Teachers, to whom I bow and am deeply indebted:

Baba Muktananda, and the Siddha Yoga tradition, from whom, in 1973, I first received the profound knowing that I am loved, and whose Presence and Love in my own Life throughout my life have been an anchor.

Werner Erhard and the coaches at Landmark, with whom, between 1972 and 1990, I participated in and led conversations that opened me, and so many others, to Transformation: choice, freedom, and Possibility, and my own power to make a difference in the lives of others.

Arnold Siegel, a pragmatic philosopher, whose teaching allowed me to anchor myself in my philosophical voice as my husband moved through the challenge of cancer, and through whom I discovered that I could find out what I think, originally, through writing.

Oscar Ichazo and The Arica School, where I discovered that many paths could lead to the same place.

Steven Pontes, whose clarity, integrity, generosity, and Service provided a platform on which I could stand and create an ending in my life that was now due.

Nóirín ní Riain, writer, teacher, revered Celtic spiritual musician, the Singer of Sacred Music, my soul sister, who led me, through a Celtic tradition (a tradition distinct from any of the other pathways that have taken me to my depths), to the Sacred, and whose laughter, playfulness, depth, heart, and Voice transported my soul into a new awakening.

Sources of Inspiration: Philosophers, Thinkers, Fellow Journeyers, Authors, Poets who have influenced how I think and where I think from, and whose own work has profoundly contributed to and influenced my own:

Owen Ó Súilleabháin *and* Mícheál Ó Súilleabháin, Nóirín's sons, extraordinary brothers and musicians, whose clear, resonant voices, Creative Spirits, Generosity of Heart, and powerful invitations brought my husband and me into the spirit of Ireland through Turas D'Anam, "Journey of the Soul," and grounded me in the land, in Music, in a spiritual tradition other than my own, and in poetry that provides openings into life as a pilgrimage. They, along with their mother, gave me access to standing for a Creative aspect of myself I had been aware of, and yet, not embraced as a calling prior to meeting them. I acknowledge Owen, in particular, for being a profound and imaginative genius and partner, encouraging me to rise to the occasion of expressing my own artistry and personal journeying into the world through this new medium; this book would not have existed had I not met him. And, I give deep gratitude for Mícheál's impish, radical, brave character and supremely powerful, poetic, as well as musical, voice which transports me to new territories of depth and thought.

Mark Nepo, whose voice has allowed me and so many others to come to ground with ourselves, to embrace our humanity as that which brings us into Heart, into our True Selves, and whose poetry touches and awakens the conscious mind, bringing us to new healings.

David Whyte, whose pioneer spirit and brilliance as a poet and prose author open up new horizons of vulnerability, Courage, and Insight, carrying us into distances we could not see on our own.

Keith Taylor, Artist in Residence at Isle Royale National Park in 2019, whose generosity of heart, giving ways, straightforwardness of character, and sharing of his incredible poetry inspired my own writing during the summer most of these poems were written.

John O'Donohue, who brings me into Wonder, and whose capacity for creating Blessings, for naming and distinguishing all the spaces the human heart enters validates our Soul Life, thus bringing us to being at one with ourselves.

Parker Palmer, whose voice of Courage, depth of humor, self-compassion, and understanding of Teaching from who we are have opened up territory to simply *be*.

Eckart Tolle, whose words bring us to Stillness , and to Awakening to our own Greater Intelligence, outside of our small and petty minds.

Dawna Markova, who opens us to our own nature, and the criticality of distinguishing our individuality in such a way that we find, express, and shape ourselves and our lives.

Mary Oliver, whose amazing poetry in which she captures life's details brings us into our capacity for wonder and astonishment at being with and appreciating the everyday.

Jodie Hollander, whose three-hour workshop on Ekphrastic poetry opened pathways for me to re-member the small details of poetry writing that brings poetry into music.

For my dearest Friends and Contributing Partners in the Parenting Journey:

Sandy Robbins, my dear, dear friend and former colleague, who carved a clear path for our daughter to create and live into her own transformation as she steps ever more boldly into living the life she is now creating.

My many parenting friends, whose wise wisdom, generous Heart listening, sometimes coaching, and sometimes merely "being there" provided companionship, support, strength, resiliency, knowing that I was not alone in my parenting journey: Sheila Strom, Mary Scribner, Susan Allen, Peg Gale, Anna Young, Mary Harrigan, Irene Pecenco, Naomi Siegel, Dave Beck, Joanne Hopkins, Ruth Blaney, and Pat Colgan.

For my father and my mother, who taught me the art of self-discipline as a foundation for fulfilment.

And finally, for my daughter, who has been my teacher throughout her life, through whom I deeply learned compassion, surrender, and heart pathways for staying connected as we, now, walk our journeys side by side.

Photo Credits:

All the photos were taken at Isle Royale National Park by Amba and Don Gale with the exception of the following:

Page 83: Photo of the Old Ferryman, Lough Derg, Ireland, who takes pilgrims to Inis Caeltra (Holy Island)

Page 100: Water color of Gale Cabin by Elizabeth Kemmer, Don's grandmother's best friend at Isle Royale

Page 154: View from our home, Bainbridge Island, Washington

Page 159: Moonrise from our deck, Bainbridge Island, Washington

Discover more about Amba Gale's work, through www.galeleadership.com, including her other poetry and prose writings, the opportunities for transformation and awakening through coaching, workshops, course work, and retreats, and a particular course, Crossing Thresholds, The Next Opening, which is based on this book.

About the Author

Amba is a teacher, coach, and guide for people and businesses, primarily through interactive coaching conversations, opening territory for people to live an alive, awakened, conscious, loving, mindful, fulfilled life.

As a devoted adventurer of inner and outer travels, a pioneer and pilgrim dedicated to personal development, to making a difference in the lives of human beings, she is committed to plumbing her own depths, stepping ever more powerfully beyond what is familiar and safe. She has been designing and leading deep dives into authenticity, integrity, forgiveness, commitment, communication, collaboration, and community with others since the early seventies.

Amba received her BA from the University of California at Berkeley as a Phi Beta Kappa, majoring in English and minoring in Music. She earned a masters in music education, and began her career teaching high school English, winning an award for innovative development from the California Teachers Association. She later completed the Mastery of Management Program at Darden College. In her late twenties, she turned her attention to another kind of education: transformative learning, where developmental, ontological, poetic, and philosophical conversations contribute to the opening of the human eyes, the opening into Awareness.

Amba is the founder of Gale Leadership Development, through whose clearing she opens the space for people to take a powerful and authentic inward journey, touching their authentic selves, coming into their Awareness, Wakefulness, Joy, and Aliveness, as they grow and touch ever more deeply the depths of their own Being, and see and experience their connectedness with others.

She has been writing poetry throughout her life, and weaves many of the themes of her poetry through her interactive transformational work with people. This is her first book of published poetry.

Made in the USA
Columbia, SC
24 July 2021